Wheat Country

Grant Heilman

WHEAT COUNTRY

Illustrated with one hundred twenty-four photographs by the author

THE STEPHEN GREENE PRESS

BRATTLEBORO, VERMONT

Copyright © 1977 by Grant Heilman

This book has been produced in the United States of America: designed by Aldren A. Watson, composed by American Book–Stratford Press, printed by Rapoport Printing Corporation, and bound by A. Horowitz and Son.

It is published by The Stephen Greene Press, Brattleboro, Vermont 05301.

LIBRARY OF CONGRESS CATALOGING IN PUBLICATION DATA

Heilman, Grant, 1919–
  Wheat country.

  1. Wheat trade — United States — Pictorial works.
I. Title.
  HD9049.W5U4295   338.1′7′3110973   76–13814

ISBN 0-8289-0281-X

Frontispiece and title page photos: WALLA WALLA, WASHINGTON

Contents

Two minor terminology problems need to be straightened out lest they lead to chaos.

The first is international. In the United States, wheat is a specific series of plants of the genus *Triticum,* and corn is a totally different plant, of the genus *Zea.*

In English-speaking countries other than the United States, the term "corn" can mean simply the seeds of the main cereal crop of a particular region. It refers to small grains, including wheat but sometimes also barley or oats. What the United States calls "corn" is known in those countries as "maize."

Many versions of the Bible use the term "corn," but actually refer to small grains, usually but not always wheat. The King James version of the Bible uses both the words "wheat" and "corn" as translations for the same Hebrew word. Corn as maize was unknown in the Biblical areas.

So, for purposes of this book I stick to the United States usage, in which wheat is "wheat," and corn is "corn," as in maize.

The second problem is domestic. In the United States, sorghum—a crop slightly similar to corn—is known in some places as "milo," others as "sorghum," and still a few others as "maize." The tendency is to standardize on "sorghum," so I've used that throughout the book; but both "milo" and "maize" are still in common usage throughout much of the farm country.

To the American Farmer

For most of my adult life I've had an ongoing love affair with the American farmer.

It's included the Texan who found me examining his sorghum field one morning and said: "Shoot, come on along and I'll show you a *real* field." Off we went in his pickup, and it turned out the other field was a hundred miles away.

And a young black man in North Carolina who pulled a lath of tobacco out of a curing shed and said: "That's the best leaf I've ever seen, and I was the one who grew it."

And the gray-haired Kansan who stood with me watching his son drive a giant new Steiger tractor and twelve-row corn planter across a mile-long field. "That rig cost $35,000," he told me, "and it's paid for, and so is the field. You know, I started out without enough cash to buy glass for the windows in the shack we rented. That first winter we just tacked in heavy paper, and somehow we managed."

What the American farmer has, I long ago concluded, is pride. While it is he who gets pleasure from pride in what he is doing, it is the whole world that shares in the results.

The Grain

A little background

Wheat is grown in more parts of the world, and manages to produce successfully under more varied conditions, than any other crop. It's the farmer's handy dandy standby.

In the eastern United States and Europe, rainfall of forty to fifty inches a year is common, and wheat flourishes under these damp conditions. But it can skimp along on twelve to fifteen inches a year also, uncomplaining and doggedly productive.

Yields in eastern Colorado may drop to twenty bushels to the acre in areas where rainfall hovers at twelve to fifteen inches. And two hundred miles away, on the Western Slope area of Colorado, the New Gaines varieties are growing under irrigation, with plenty of water, poured on at optimum times, and production soars to more than a hundred bushels. Given a choice, the wheat does best in fifteen to thirty-five inches of rain, and a temperate climate. But it's an adaptable, workhorse crop, and every month of the year it's being harvested somewhere in the world.

Planting with two double drills. INGALLS, KANSAS

9

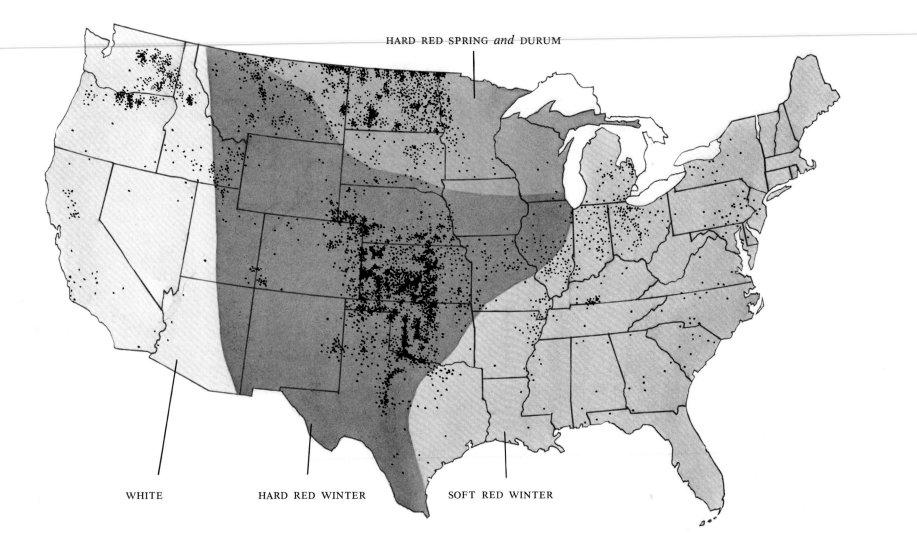

HARD RED SPRING *and* DURUM

WHITE   HARD RED WINTER   SOFT RED WINTER

*Distribution of the five classes of wheat in the United States
harvest of 1969. Each dot on this map represents 10,000 acres;
the total wheat acreage harvested in that year was 45,372,868.*
SOURCE: *United States Department of Commerce*

The biggest producers of wheat are the USSR, followed by the United States, China, France, Canada, Argentina, and Australia, usually in that order.

In recent years much of the United States' production has been exported, sometimes reaching almost 70 percent. Whereas fifteen years ago wheat had been a major American farm problem because of the gigantic surpluses that were piled up in our storage bins, now the carryover is perilously low. In 1960 we had a massive 1,313 million bushels in storage. By 1974 the carryover had dropped to 247.4 million bushels, less than one-fifth that of 1960, and certainly not enough to cushion the United States or the world against lean years. This has ramifications not only for a potentially hungry world, but also for a world that is intensely political. The stockpile seems to have been rebuilt somewhat following the 1976 crop, but there's little likelihood of our seeing giant surpluses stored again.

One of the reasons wheat is so adaptable is that it has had so long to adapt. There are some 200,000 species of flowering plants known to man; about 3,000 of these have been used for food, but only about 200 have been domesticated. The grasses are among the major contributors, for they include wheat and other grains, rice, corn, and sugar cane. More than 70 percent of our farmland is devoted to cereals, grasses that yield edible grains.

But of the thousands of food plants, wheat and barley were the first of the grains that the wandering families of the prehistoric era collected. No one knows how long ago wheat was gathered by man—or by woman—from the wild grasses. There is evidence that ancestral strains of cultivated wheat existed in the early Stone Age (Upper Paleolithic). Milling equipment of a crude sort has been discovered which is believed to date back 75,000 years. The earliest actual remains of grain date from about 5,000 B.C., and archaeologists are able to distinguish between wild wheat and early cultivated wheat.

It seems likely it was at least as late as 10,000 B.C. before wheat was other than a wild grass, sought after by early man forced to follow animal herds and wild plants. At some time after 10,000 B.C., man took the giant step forward that changed him from a nomad and hunter to an agriculturist with a permanent home. This transition took place at no specific time, for it extended over several millennia in different parts of the world, and is still going on in a few remote spots.

It's unclear how he, or she, first discovered that if a few seeds were put into the ground at the right time under the right conditions they would grow and return a great dividend. Looking backward it's easy enough to build up many theories about it.

But the individuals who discovered crop cultivation probably had no concept of its importance. In all likelihood they just learned that it could simplify their lives, not that it would completely change the way of living of the entire world.

Today, products made from wheat provide the basic diet for more of the world's people than do those of any other

crop. Wheat's only competitor is rice, geographically restricted in its production because of its need for large quantities of controllable water, but still producing 85 percent as many tons as wheat.

Because of its widespread cultivation and its long history of usefulness, wheat has developed into thousands of varieties. In the United States probably about two hundred varieties are grown commercially, each specifically adapted to available rainfall, soil conditions, disease resistance, market demand, and dozens of other criteria. Hybrid wheat, far behind corn in development because of genetic problems, is on the market in limited quantities, and promises to set off a major increase in wheat yields, though not so dramatic a difference as hybridization of corn made forty years ago.

The United States varieties are grouped into five classes, according to the kind of flour they produce. The class is determined by the hardness of the kernel, the color of the kernel, and the planting time. The kernel's color has no effect on the quality of the wheat or its use in flour; it is used merely to identify the variety.

There are Hard Red Winter Wheat, and Hard Red Spring. These are high in protein and are used for bread flour. Durum Wheat, the hardest and also high in protein, provides semolina and durum flour, which go into macaroni, spaghetti, and noodles—the pasta products. And finally, the soft wheats—Soft Red Winter and White—provide flour for cakes, pastries, crackers, and many of the snack and breakfast foods.

Some two hundred varieties of wheat are in use in the United States. New varieties, including hybrids, are constantly being added. HALFVILLE, PENNSYLVANIA

Different varieties of mature wheat heads

Maturing kernels on stalk

Most of the wheat produced in Western Europe is Soft Wheat. Italy, as might be expected, produces Durum Wheat for pasta purposes, although Durum represents only about a third of its wheat production. The USSR produces both hard and soft wheats.

The term "Winter" or "Spring" refers to the time of year in which the grain is planted. Spring Wheat, obviously, is planted in the spring. Its seed and young growth are delicate and would not stand cold winters. Almost all Spring Wheat is grown across the northern edge of the wheat belt, in northern Montana, the Dakotas, and Minnesota. Planted mostly in May, it's harvested in August and September of the same year.

Winter Wheat is something of a misnomer. It really means the grain is planted during the fall months, usually September and October, grows to four to eight inches in the fall before freezing, and remains in the ground during the winter, its root system well established. The tops may be pastured off by cattle during the fall, winter, or spring, but the plant survives and regrows. Harvest of Winter Wheat runs from May, in Arizona and Texas, to September along the Canadian border states.

In general, the hard wheats are grown in the wheat belt states—usually considered as Kansas, Oklahoma, Texas, Nebraska, Colorado, Montana, North Dakota, South Dakota, and Minnesota. White Wheat grows in the west coast states, especially the fabulous Palouse wheat country of eastern Washington. The Soft Red Winter Wheat is grown mostly in the eastern half of the United States.

Kernels after combining

15

Although each of the various types of wheat has its particular end use, that's not quite the whole story. Since about 70 percent of our wheat production is exported, it's clear that in foreign countries bread represents a much more vital part of the diet than in the United States. Bread and hard roll annual consumption figures per person, taken from a *New York Times* article, look like this:

United States	80 POUNDS
West Germany	120
USSR	525

Bread is, as the ads say, basic. But it's obviously more basic in Russia than it is here. As a result, it is a major source of protein, and foreign countries look especially at the protein content. Here in the United States bread is not usually considered a vital protein source. But there are two interesting factors here: first, in the United States bread is usually fortified with a number of chemical additives to make it more important as a source of vitamins and minerals, but it isn't fortified with protein. And second, the protein content in bread is a major factor in how it can be processed and baked. If protein is inadequate, the bread won't hold its shape, automatic forming machinery gets messed up, and the bread collapses on the grocer's shelf. Thus the protein content of wheat becomes a major influence on its desirability both here and abroad. But the protein content goes up and down in various years, depending on weather, quantities of fertilizer used, height of the grain stalks, and a host of relatively unknown factors: It is not easily controlled.

The result of this is that protein content becomes a part of the pricing structure of wheat, in addition to the grain's type and grade. In a year of poor protein quality, higher protein wheats bring a premium which becomes an important part of the price. In the 1975 harvest, for example, an increase in protein in Hard Red Winter Wheat from 11 to 14 percent meant at times an added fifty cents per bushel. In a year in which protein content is uniformly higher, premiums are likely to be lower.

The performances of test plots like this one are basic to decisions on the effectiveness of new varieties.
GRAND JUNCTION, COLORADO

Wheat Country

Where it is, and why

What controls agriculture in much of the United States is the availability of water. The desert will literally bloom, provided it gets water. We can talk of soil quality and temperatures, but water is vital.

With plenty of moisture wheat grows beautifully. But it can also manage with very little. That's its success story. The new varieties will grow a hundred bushels to the acre in irrigated country where there is the equivalent of forty inches of rain. The irrigated acres will grow anything, but there are few of them, and around them stretch miles of dryness. It's out on the dry land, where rain may total less than twenty inches, that wheat is the queen. Nothing else does well, and there are millions of acres of this dry country.

Agriculturists tend to think of the "humid" east and the "dry" west. A number of artificial lines have been set up to distinguish the two areas. Sometimes the eastern boundaries of the Dakotas, Nebraska, Kansas, Oklahoma, and Texas are considered the dividing line, sometimes the 100th

WELD COUNTY, COLORADO

STERLING, KANSAS

Out here, where rainfall may total
less than twenty inches a year,
wheat is queen.

GREELEY, COLORADO

For use in hilly wheat-growing spots (here, the Palouse Country of eastern Washington near Lacrosse), manufacturers provide special "hillside" combines. Hydraulic levelers keep the combine body level as it goes across the hill—as if a cow could sprout longer legs on one side when she pastures a hillside. The header on the front of the combine, which cuts and collects the grain, is on a swivel so it can follow the contour of the hill even though the combine body is level.

21

Modern techniques reduce the time necessary to harvest one acre to 37 minutes. And most modern combine cabs are air-conditioned. KANSAS, NEAR COLBY

meridian, which comes about halfway through these states. Others have made it the twenty-inch rainfall line, which wanders in and out near the other two lines.

But it's really much more vague. It's related to too many factors to tie down: soil, wind, altitude—and farmers' attitudes.

The effect of decreasing rainfall is all there to see, along U.S. Route 36, across the northern edge of Missouri and Kansas, and into Colorado. In Missouri the fields are corn and soybeans. They take plenty of moisture.

Cross the Missouri at St. Joe and drive west into the gentle hills of northern Kansas. There's still mostly corn, on the hillsides and the bottomlands too. Then, as you continue west, an occasional field of sorghum shows up on the hilltops where less moisture accumulates. Sorghum needs less rain than corn. Then, gradually, corn becomes common only on the bottomlands, where runoff from rainfall boosts the moisture in the soil; the hillsides are sorghum. Then wheat appears on the hilltops, and corn disappears even from the bottomlands, replaced by sorghum.

As the flatness of western Kansas stretches before you, both corn and sorghum have disappeared, and there are only fields of dry pasture, and wheat.

Finally, when you've crossed into eastern Colorado, you come on summer fallow, the farming technique of the really dry country. Wheat is farmed in strips of land, and each strip is planted only every other year. In alternate

24

Among Pennsylvania's Amish, there are still farms where the grain is cut with a horse-drawn binder. Stacked by hand to dry, the wheat is then loaded on wagons and brought to a centrally located, *steam-driven thresher. Each acre harvested using fifty-year-old techniques like these takes more than 12 hours of stifling, itchy, exhausting work.* SOUTH OF CHURCHTOWN, PENNSYLVANIA

MYERSTOWN, PENNSYLVANIA

years the unplanted strip is cultivated to keep weeds down, but not cropped, so its moisture can accumulate. Two years' moisture is needed to produce a single crop.

"Wheat yields here go from zero to forty bushels an acre," a Colorado farmer told me. "Some years we make real money, others we just plow it down and don't bother to harvest. It's all a great gamble, with the odds set by God."

A few places in the United States, but especially in Lancaster County, in Pennsylvania, the Amish people still harvest wheat as it was done by everyone fifty years ago.

They cut the grain, using horses to pull their binders. They stack by hand to dry the wheat, then they load it onto wagons and bring it to a central spot where it is threshed with a steam-driven threshing machine.

Picturesque and beautiful, threshing also carries with it an exorbitant labor cost. A study of labor times in threshing techniques similar to those used by the Amish showed it took more than twelve hours of labor to harvest an acre of wheat. By contrast, Kansas State University did a study of labor requirements to harvest an acre of wheat in the big country of western Kansas in 1975, and found harvest labor time was thirty-seven minutes!

"The romance of threshing," an elderly Kansan told me one day as we examined the rusting remains of a threshing machine, "was great. But it was really stifling, itchy, exhausting work. I'll take an air-conditioned combine cab anytime."

25

Patterns

A view from the air

From the air, the farmlands of the United States constantly amaze me with their patterns. In the rolling hilly country, crops are increasingly planted in strips that follow the contours of the hills, so that in effect the crop rows are on the level. Soil Conservation Service and County Agricultural Agents help the farmer lay out his fields on contour by walking across a sloping field carrying a hand level, using the level to place staked flags level in relation to a fixed base point. When the farmer plows, he keeps his tractor level by following the contour flags.

The purpose of strip cropping and contouring under these conditions is to minimize erosion caused by heavy rainfall. A rule of thumb in conservation is that contouring will cut soil loss by half—though this will of course vary. In east-

ern Pennsylvania, soil loss on "up and down" farming may reach seven tons of soil per acre per year; contouring will cut that to three to four tons per acre.

In the dry wheat country of the very light rainfall areas— Colorado, Wyoming, Montana, and North Dakota are good examples—most of the wheat is fallow farmed. That is, a crop is grown only every other year on any strip of land, to conserve moisture.

Combiners can set their machines to scatter the straw behind them, or to lay it down in neat rows. If it's going to be baled and kept for animal bedding, it's dropped into neat rows—windrowing, it's called.

North of Williston, North Dakota, it's summer fallow,
the farming technique for the really dry country.

27

FACING PAGE: *Strip cropping on the contour west of The Buck,*
Lancaster County, Pennsylvania. Here, following the contours
can reduce soil loss through erosion from seven tons to three
or four tons per acre per year.

In Weld County, Colorado, it takes two years' moisture to
produce a crop. So you plant alternate strips of land in
alternate years, and cultivate the intervening strips to keep
the weeds down and save the precious moisture.

29

30   *Wheat yields here go from zero to forty bushels an acre—*
it's a gamble on odds set by God. WELD COUNTY, COLORADO

If the straw is going to be baled and kept for animal bedding,
the combines are set to drop it in windrows. KANAPOLIS, KANSAS

NORTH OF MCPHERSON, KANSAS

Facing page: ALDEN, KANSAS

Planting and Growing

Busy, in Arlington, Kansas

*Getting ready for planting,
with 28-foot double offset disks
behind a four-wheel-drive tractor.* COPELAND, KANSAS

Getting wheat into the ground at the right time is almost as touchy as getting it harvested. If the moisture's too low, it won't germinate; if it's too high the planter bogs down and gets clogged. When it's just right, everyone stops whatever they're doing, and plants.

Out in the dry country you hope for moisture for growing—even the dew counts. And in winter you pray for snow. It not only provides moisture, but without it the wind loosens the soil, blows it away from the roots, and the plants pull out of the ground or freeze. With good snow cover the wheat just huddles there, comfortable and protected, ready to start pushing in the spring.

Cattle can gain a lot of weight on wheat pasture. Best of all, you can still harvest the grain. The cattle chew it to the ground and it grows right back.

Eventually, the wheat heads up, and when the heads add their weight to the stalk, the plants begin to ripple in the wind. There's nothing quite so beautiful.

35

KENNESON, NEBRASKA

You pull a forty-foot drill and you're putting in more than fifteen acres of wheat every hour you're on that tractor. Out here you just about go from horizon to horizon before you have to turn. It's pretty dull work, but you get a lot of grain in. If you figure it at four minutes to the acre, you're putting in about a million seeds to each acre, so that's 250,000 seeds every minute. INGALLS, KANSAS

38

When the moisture's right,
stop what you're doing and PLANT.
WEST OF JOHNSON, KANSAS

In the dry country,
you pray for moisture for growing—
even the dew helps.

39

40

And in the winter you pray for snow—to keep the soil around the roots, to keep the plants from freezing—so the wheat just stays huddled and comfortable, waiting for spring. ABBYVILLE, KANSAS

When the plants begin to ripple in the wind,
there's nothing quite so beautiful.

41

Wheat pasture can put a lot of weight on cattle—
and you can still harvest the grain. HAPPY, TEXAS

They eat it down, and it comes right back. KRESS, TEXAS

43

Trials and Tribulations

It's not so easy as it seems

NARDIN, OKLAHOMA

It's not all so easy as it seems. A lot can happen on the way from the planter to the combine. City people think it just grows; country people know differently.

"A wheat crop's like a cat," a grower told me as we examined his crop, flattened by rain. "It's got nine lives. The great thing is, it almost always manages to muddle through. We do a lot of worryin' along the way, though."

"What a wheat farmer really prays for is damp weather for planting, wet weather for growing, dry weather for harvest. But while he's at it, he also prays for snow during the winter, and for no hailstorms after the wheat heads up. But there's so many things to worry about, that's only the beginnin' of your prayin'."

Because wheat does better with less water than any other major crop, the temptation is always to plant it where there may not be enough water even for wheat. So, really, the major problem is drought. COLFAX, WASHINGTON

45

The answer to the moisture problem is irrigation, like this "center pivot" rig, since the difference between irrigated wheat and dry-land wheat can be the difference between a big profit and no crop at all. But, if there's irrigation water available, chances are the farmer will find a crop that returns more money for his water investment than wheat does. NEAR CENTER, COLORADO

Planting patterns in the snow are beautiful, but they spell danger to the wheat man. He needs a solid snow cover to protect his wheat during the winter months. And of course, the more snow there is, the more water is available when the snow melts.

But when there's hail, there's nothing to do but wait for next year's crop. Hail takes the head right off. Your crop's lying on the ground, and there's no way to sweep it up. What's worse, the closer to harvest, the greater the damage.

SOUTH OF SMITH CENTER, KANSAS

47

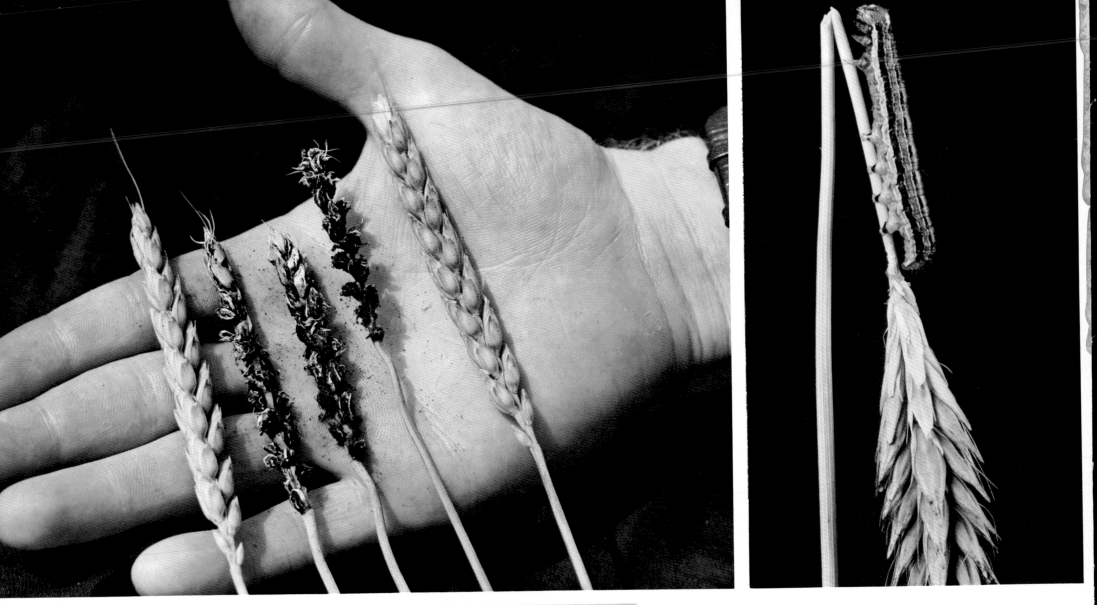

There are diseases like smut,
and insects like army worms.
When the wheat looks bad,
you've got to fly on chemicals.

"There's a lot of chewed fingernails when a cloud comes up at harvest time. I seen a storm come across a field just as the combines was comin' in. When it quit hailin' five minutes later there wasn't any grain left to combine." SOUTH OF ABERDEEN, SOUTH DAKOTA

48

KANSAS RADIO ANNOUNCER: *I never saw a rain like that one this afternoon. It left roads blocked and fields flooded and it'll take a couple of days just to know how much damage it really did. It was a real soaker.*

You're always pushing to get your combines into the field because you're afraid of hail. But you get them there too soon after a rain, and you've got trouble. Pulling $35,000 worth of combine out of a mudhole isn't any fun.
NARDIN, OKLAHOMA

You breathe easier when the combining's over, but you aren't through yet. Granary weevils, if you store your own wheat, can leave you sitting there with just the shells left. If you sell your grain fast, then that's someone else's problem.

51

Urban families who drive through farm country on their vacations are always struck by what they refer to as "the abandoned farms." Truth is, there are a lot of abandoned farm houses, but almost no abandoned farms. The land is still being farmed, but fewer people are needed to farm it. Forty years ago, when wheat went in with a six-foot-wide drill, it took one man to plant it. Now, when it goes in with a forty-foot drill, it still takes one man, but he gets six—almost seven—times as much planted.

So one family can handle greater acreage—and some farmers have been forced to move to the city. But the land of those who move isn't idle; it's taken over by a neighbor anxious to expand to take advantage of the power of big equipment.

While the farm population dwindled during the past fifty years from more than half of the total population to 4 percent, there has been a ripple effect as well. Thousands of small crossroads towns depended on the purchases of surrounding farmers. When the farm population dwindled, many of the small towns died. This was aided by the increased mobility of farmers as cars and roads got better. They were willing to go fifteen or twenty miles to town, rather than three or four.

It's hard to say exactly why some small towns withered, and others bloomed, but that's the way it worked. Some have empty streets, others have parking problems. ARGONIA, KANSAS

54

COTTONWOOD FALLS, KANSAS

Harvest: The Climax

Speed, long days, excitement, fatigue

Rusting threshers, south of Franklin, Nebraska

The harvest's come a long way, from the gathering by hand of a few bundles of wild grasses, the grain to be beaten free. A long way even from fifty years ago, when horse-drawn reaper-binders cut the stalks and bound them into bundles which were then carried to a massive threshing machine which separated the grain.

Gone is the thresher, replaced by the combine. As its name indicates, the combine does a combination of jobs. It cuts the stalks, separates the grain from the stalks, spews the stalks back onto the ground in a neat row (or broadcast, as the farmer prefers), puts the grain into a storage bin and eventually pumps it from the bin into a truck. It does all this, including the unloading, while lumbering across a rough field. And, probably most important, it does it all operated by only one person.

It is, truly, an incredible machine, a combination of wheels, belts, gears, pulleys, motors, and pumps. It snorts, purrs, roars, thumps, bumps, and whooshes.

But these are expensive monsters, so expensive that individual farmers can scarcely justify owning them for a couple of weeks' work each year. Thus, "custom" combiners travel the wheat belt, keeping their machines busy and producing income for as long as six months of each year.

These modern nomads come equipped with the newest in combines—the big operators trade them at least every two years. They also come with fancy house trailers, sparkling trucks, college boys as labor, and two-way radios to maintain communications.

It's romantic, wending your way from Texas to Canada along the wheat trail—but it's hard work too, with unlimited hours in the field, dust, storms, tension, and the constant moving.

Many combiners cut on the same farms year after year. I was on a farm in western Nebraska a couple of years ago when the combines and trucks all stopped for a few minutes for a birthday celebration, complete with a cake brought out to the field. The occasion was the sixteenth birthday of one of the combiner's daughters. She was driving a truck. The cake was baked by the wheat farmer's wife.

"It's hard to believe," the girl's mother told me, "but when we first came here to combine I had just been married. I've been back here every single year since, even when I was pregnant. We're all the best of friends, even if we only see each other once a year."

SOUTHERN MONTANA

"Sights like this one from the early 1950's are limited to back roads these days. You just can't bunch this many combines on an interstate highway. But combiners get to know each other, and they enjoy traveling in groups. They'll join together to bid jobs, and complain to each other when there're too many combines and too few acres. It's a big investment, and those machines have to keep running to make a payout." BRIDGEPORT, NEBRASKA

Combine operators come from all areas of the wheat belt. Some work only in nearby neighbors' fields. Others make combining a total career. One little town in Kansas—Buhler—puts almost a hundred people on the road each year.

"My dad started in 1946, first year after World War II. There were almost all dirt roads in farm country then, and he churned through the dusty roads with a six-foot Gleaner and a John Deere tractor pulling it.

"I was seven, and I've been at it ever since. We've got MF 750's and 760's now, and there are eighteen of us traveling together. Oh, yeah, three dogs too.

"Our Massey 760 has a twenty-four-foot header, but I hear they're workin' on thirty-foot headers. We'll be standin' in line for them when they come out.

"We go clear to the Canadian border, starting in Texas. Then we go back down to Texas and Oklahoma to combine beans and sorghum, and we aren't through until in November sometime. We're ready to start up again early in May."

A big operator will start in Texas in mid-May, working clear to the northern end of Montana, or even into Canada, by September. Then he may put on a corn or sorghum attachment and take his equipment back south to Oklahoma and Texas for another month or two of work. If he has school-age children, his family usually joins him when school's out, goes back home when school starts in the fall.

It's the way unloading the circus at each small town used to be. Every time you come into a new area you've got to take the headers off the trucks, roll the combines off, and somehow get the two together, greased, fueled, and ready to go. I guess the combines are the present-day circus elephants. STERLING, KANSAS

Operated by only one man, the modern combine does the work that fifty years ago took the labor of perhaps twelve to fifteen men and as many or more animals. It cuts the wheat, separates the grain from the straw, then separates the grain from the remaining chaff, blows the straw and chaff back out onto the field again ready for baling as animal bedding or for plowing under, stores 150 bushels of threshed grain in its bin, and on demand pumps its load into a truck for delivery to the country elevator—all without stopping, all without getting thirsty or tired or hungry. And its cab is air-conditioned.

60

61

Finally, the day comes, and you look at the sky, worry about a little cloud forming down at the horizon. The radio is on wherever you go, with the grain market reports every hour, and weather advisories in between.

You keep walking into the fields. Experience tells you where the wheat will dry out fastest. You pull off a couple of heads of wheat, run them through your fingers to feel how the grain separates. You chew on the kernels to gauge the toughness.

And you wait. You go over the combine with a grease gun for the hundredth time, and wait. Finally, you convince everyone—they aren't difficult to convince—that you ought to cut a swath. Your wife sighs with relief; if you get started you won't be so grouchy.

You cut into the field. You can feel the moisture in the stalks, but you cut anyhow. The combine sounds normal, same wheezes as last year. Then you roll back to where the trucks are parked, and you stop. Someone climbs up on top with the coffee can and dips the wheat sample.

LOVELAND, COLORADO   WINDSOR, COLORADO

The elevators are waiting for the morning rush, which gets under way only slowly because the dew has to evaporate from the wheat before the combines can start. It's a time when everyone waits anxiously.

You drive to the elevator in town. Everyone wants to go along, but no one has much to say on the ride, the tension's too heavy. Lots of other farmers are there already. The sample testing takes only a minute or two.

Moisture's still too high—16 percent, and they're insisting on 14 percent without a docking price. You talk it over with the others, sipping coffee, marking time. Someone drives in with a truckload; his earlier sample was OK. Everyone crowds around while the machine weighs up the sample and the lights flash 13.8 percent—he's in safe!

There's a lot of hurry up and wait. You run a sample cut, then sit around waiting to get the results of the moisture test. That's when the tension builds. While you're waiting you find time to move a young rabbit out of the way of the combines and trucks.

FACING PAGE:
Left and bottom, NARDIN, OKLAHOMA
Upper right, WINDSOR, COLORADO

WINDSOR, COLORADO

65

*You drive back home, and again—for the hundred-and-first time—
you check the combine with a grease gun. And you wait, worn out
without working, for another two hours before you go through the
same sequence again.*

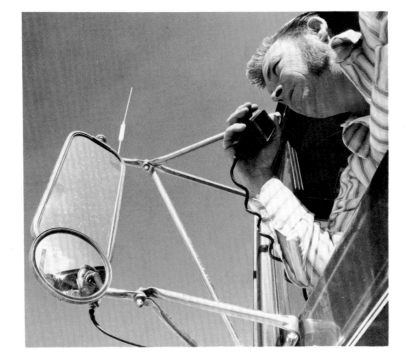

*This time you make it. The sun and prairie wind have done their
work, and your moisture's dropped enough. You come back out of
the elevator office, pick up the radio microphone in your truck,
and tell them back in the fields to get the combines rolling. The
harvest season is on!*

Back in the fields, they're waiting for the sun to shine hotter, for the wind to blow through the wheat long enough, for the radio to come to life—for something to HAPPEN.

STERLING, KANSAS

And then, with a squawk and a rush of static, the word comes. The combiners bolt like jackrabbits into their cabs. The machines cough, then roar, then lumber toward the cut edge of the test swath. And the hot, itchy dust begins to fly.

WINDSOR, COLORADO

Once you're running, it becomes a kind of managerial game, to keep everything going smoothly. The trucks have to be on hand to empty the combines . . . the ground has to be examined to see the combines aren't missing grain . . . fuel has to get to the combines . . . you have to keep an eye out for your worst enemy, field fires . . . your drivers have to have some rest— but not too much. NARDIN, OKLAHOMA

It's not uncommon to see a hundred thousand dollars worth of equipment moving through a field. STERLING, KANSAS

Most agreements between combiners and farmers call for payment at an agreed-on rate per acre, plus a bonus of a few cents per bushel for every bushel per acre over some figure. In the 1976 harvest, a typical midwest figure was $8 per acre, plus 10 cents a bushel for everything over 20 bushels to the acre. The incentive figure, of course, makes the combiner anxious to do as thorough a job as possible in a field.

This is what it's all about: the investment, the sweat, the waiting, the wakening at night when a storm blows across your fields. It's all about the harvest.

Women's lib hasn't reached the wheat fields very much yet. One girl driving a truck loaded with wheat complained to me: "My daddy lets me drive this truck, but he won't let me handle the combine. He claims that's man's work, and my younger brother runs it. All the controls are power operated, the cab's air conditioned, and I'm as good a mechanic as any of my brothers. But Daddy's the boss, so I drive this damned truck."

NARDIN, OKLAHOMA

Somehow, everyone has to be fed without slowing down operations too much. That's your wife's department. Usually she has to bring two meals a day to the field, and you get fed with as little down time as possible.

GREELEY, COLORADO

75

NORTH OF JOHNSTOWN, COLORADO

NARDIN, OKLAHOMA

NARDIN, OKLAHOMA

The afternoon lineup begins. That's when everyone gets edgy all over again. The trucks can't get unloaded immediately, the combines have to shut down because they have no place to unload their grain, the combine operator frets because he makes money only when his machines are running. The elevator manager frets because the truck drivers are complaining, and his help worries because they're working as hard as they can but are still falling behind.

77

NARDIN, OKLAHOMA   JOHNSTOWN, COLORADO

The aim is to keep the grain flowing along the whole line.
When it all goes smoothly, the air is full of enthusiasm.
But if the system stumbles, blood pressures rise.

79

ARLINGTON, KANSAS

A friend of mine came back from a farmer's tour of Russia a few years back. They'd been on a collective farm in the Ukraine during the wheat harvest. Promptly at five o'clock the combine operators brought the machines to the edge of the field, got off, and walked down the road toward their homes.

"Where are they going?" he asked the collective manager.

"Home," was the reply. "It's quitting time."

My friend couldn't believe it. "Quitting time during harvest on my place," he explained to the Russian, "is when the moisture content of the grain gets so high the elevators won't store it. That's often two or three in the morning."

NARDIN, OKLAHOMA

81

*The elevators stay open
as long as the delivery trucks
keep rolling.* CALDWELL, KANSAS

YUMA, COLORADO

83

The elevators' problems run in two directions. They've got to keep taking in grain, but they can only continue to take it in if they can get rid of it, too. If the country elevator gets filled, the manager's got to quit accepting grain, and when he does, the combiners have to find another elevator, usually farther away, so they're upset. So the scramble for freight cars and over-the-highway trucks begins.
It's a juggling act.

There's a perennial shortage of grain-hauling railroad cars, and trucks, during the wheat harvest season, and only immense amounts of new capital put into the railroads are likely to remedy the problem.

*The main elevators of the
Farmers Union Grain Terminal.*
SUPERIOR, WISCONSIN

NARDIN, OKLAHOMA

85

Prairie Castles

Wheat country architecture

Except for the grain elevators, the flat horizon would stretch on endlessly. Their severe white solidity protrudes into the bright sky. These are the prairie castles.

Every wheat-country town has at least one elevator that receives grain directly from the neighboring farmers. The smaller towns are actually built around the elevators; they are the towns' reason for being.

The "country" elevators are the first collecting point. They pass their grain on to "subterminal" or "terminal" elevators, and these eventually ship it to the final users: millers, processors, exporters.

The country elevators are almost invariably located along a rail spur, and with a good highway nearby. They're a stopover point in the transportation cycle.

GRETNA, KANSAS

GARDEN CITY, KANSAS

INMAN, KANSAS

FAR-MAR-CO ELEVATOR B, HUTCHINSON, KANSAS

One of the largest elevators in the world, Far-Mar-Co Elevator B in Hutchinson, Kansas, stretches for almost half a mile. Its 1099 bins hold 18,000,000 bushels of grain. So precise is the grain handling that wheat can be stored both by quality and by variety. Low gluten wheat—gluten's the stuff that makes bread dough elastic so the final product will have fine texture—can be kept apart from high gluten.

Bucket lifts, and two miles of belt conveyor, move the wheat from trains or trucks to bins, and from one bin to another, and back to the trains and trucks. The gallery along the top of the bins is so long that employees ride bicycles through it to check bins and belts. The bins, each 127 feet high, have thermometers that constantly record the grain temperatures every six feet of bin depth, for warm wheat means decreased quality. When temperatures rise in the bins, wheat is shifted from one bin to another and examined during the process. Moving the entire contents of one of the giant bins takes less than half an hour.

LODGE GRASS, MONTANA

One day there'll be a Prairie Castle Collectors Society, members of which will hold monthly meetings and trade photographs, lore, and statistics about the early grain elevators. They may even go on field trips to visit the sites of existing relics.

It's only a matter of time until some Texas millionaire decides he should dismantle a few hundred of the old elevators and move them somewhere, like Texas, where they'll be set up as a museum. A crew will move grain from horse drawn wagons to the bins, to old railroad cars which will be pulled out of the siding by a smoking locomotive. It will be taken behind the scenes somewhere to empty its load back in the wagons so the horses can move back to the elevators again, as the new show starts for the assembled tourists.

Kids will say: "Gee, Grandpa, did you really store your wheat in those things?"

Next to tepees, they're probably the most American architecture.

Dominating the landscape at Hutchinson, Elevator B seems endless in length, and unlimited in capacity. But the wheat production of just three of Kansas' top counties would fill the entire 1099 bins in a good production year. And it is surrounded by other elevators almost as large as it is.

On the Move

Shipping, trading, ports

The story of wheat is not only the planting, growing, and harvesting, but the handling and shipping, which seem to go on endlessly. From the time the grain is cut, a series of trucks, trains, barges, and ships keeps moving it.

Practically no American wheat is consumed in the county it was grown in. All but about 30 percent of it is shipped to some foreign country for processing. So the farmer, vital as he is, is only the beginning of a complicated transportation chain.

More wheat leaves the United States through New Orleans than any other port. Duluth-Superior handles both "salties," ships actually going overseas, and "lakers," ships which will move the grain from one lake port to another.

Grain Terminal Association
cooperative elevator
at Superior, Wisconsin.

SOUTH OF HANNIBAL, MISSOURI

FACING PAGE:
Left, SOUTH CENTRAL KANSAS
Bottom, SUPERIOR, WISCONSIN
Far left, WEST OF AULT, COLORADO

SOUTH OF HANNIBAL, MISSOURI

Because of its location, the Mississippi River is a natural channel for grain transportation. In 1973, the port of Minneapolis–St. Paul, at the head of the Mississippi, loaded almost five-and-a-half million tons of grain for shipment downriver. Most of this was bound for the port of New Orleans, for overseas shipment.

Compared to other shipping techniques, river transportation is highly efficient. It takes less than a fourth as much energy to haul grain by river as it does by truck. Unfortunately, the upper river is closed by ice about three months of the year, and when time is a factor, river traffic loses out—it's slow.

The cost of barge hauling is affected by another problem. Empty barges have to come back up the river, and there is a scarcity of high-bulk cargo to carry upriver. These river barges handle immense quantities of goods. A fifty-car freight train using "big john" cars hauls about 100,000 bushels of wheat. That much will fit onto two barges, and a towboat may handle up to twenty barges, a total of a million bushels. Big trucks carry only about 800 bushels. On the other hand, of course, trucks and freight cars can be loaded at country or subterminal elevators and taken directly to final destination without unloading. Barge grain must usually be unloaded and reloaded at least once, often twice.

99

From a conversation with the first mate of a grain ship loading at Superior, Wisconsin:

"We've got a German owned ship, registered in Singapore. The Captain is Greek, the other officers are German, and most of the crew is Spanish. We were commissioned in Germany last summer. I came on board in Belgium and we went to South America to pick up a load of soybeans for Gdynia, Poland. We unloaded there and came here in ballast. We'll take on 15,000 tons of durum wheat, go out through the lakes and the St. Lawrence Seaway, and deliver the wheat to Algeria. After that, we'll have to see. . . ."

The viewpoint of a state grain inspector:

"Our job is to see to it that the purchaser, usually an official of a foreign company or government who never sees the wheat until it's dumped into his own bins in his own country, gets what he contracted for. We take frequent samples, and they're analyzed and reported on."

While most of the U.S. wheat was being given away under various governmental programs, the recipients couldn't complain much about quality. Now that most of it is being sold for hard cash, the buyer really insists on getting what he's paying for.

Of Politics and Wheat

A little mumbling, with few solutions, but some pointing out

Index of Agricultural Production

Percentage of 1961–1965 average

DEVELOPED COUNTRIES:

*North America, Europe, U.S.S.R., Japan,
Republic of South Africa, Australia, and New Zealand*

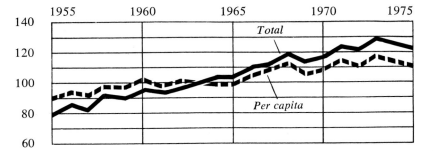

LESS DEVELOPED COUNTRIES:

*Latin America, Asia (except Japan and Communist Asia),
and Africa (except Republic of South Africa).*

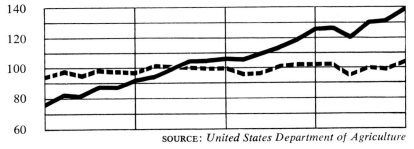

SOURCE: *United States Department of Agriculture*

*Grain ship loading at Farmers Union Grain Terminal No. 2,
Superior, Wisconsin.*

This book was hardly meant to be a technical treatise on wheat, much less a discussion ground for politics. Still, it's a kind of copout if I don't at least try to talk about some of the world's agricultural, and food, problems.

Probably the most that can be done is some pointing out. Questions are easier than answers, and are at least an invitation to the reader to search for answers. Let's look at some questions.

Will the world starve? This graph has a bearing on the answer. Essentially it shows that through 1974 the total food production of the Less Developed Countries had been growing as rapidly as that of the Developed Countries. But because the population growth of the Less Developed Countries was considerably higher, the food production per capita in the Less Developed Countries has remained about constant—their food situation is not improving.

If population continues to increase, then food production per capita must at least match it, hopefully increase faster. Most agricultural economists are pessimistic about this possibility.

Unless the world, particularly the less developed countries, agrees that limiting population is desirable, and makes a real effort to do so, in the long run large numbers of people on the planet are likely to starve.

When? I think there are too many variables to say. Two experts, in a widely read book published in 1967, *Famine 1975!,** predicted: "By 1975 a disaster of unprecedented magnitude will face the world. Famines, greater than any in history, will ravage the developed nations."

I don't believe the predicted mass famine has yet come about. But I agree with the Paddocks that it is going to come, at some future time.

Can the United States stop starvation for the rest of the world? No. We can put off the crisis, and we can produce a really incredible amount of food if our political problems don't destroy farmers' initiative.

Finally, though, sometime, unless we reach a stable population in the world very quickly—and this seems an utter impossibility to me—starvation will come.

Whatever happened to all those farm surpluses we used to have? They've been used up. In 1960 we were wallowing in a storage carryover from previous years of 1,313 million bushels of wheat, and in that year we produced an additional 1,355 million bushels. The amount already stored, then, represented virtually a year's production. In 1974,

* *Famine 1975! America's Decision, Who Will Survive?* by William and Paul Paddock, published 1967 by Little, Brown & Company, Boston.

however, although new wheat produced had risen to 1,840 million bushels, old wheat stored had shrunk to 249 million bushels—less than one-seventh of a year's production. The carryover from the 1976 crop was somewhat larger.

But we're now frightened that a bad crop year, either here or abroad, will bring on famine somewhere. The old cushion is gone.

There's an effort to establish "world" storage facilities, probably through the United Nations, but I think we're fairly far away from doing that on an international basis. Much of the feeling in the United States is that we would likely have to put up most of the money to build the storage elevators, and then would have to provide most of the grain to fill them. If we're going to do all this, the argument runs, why shouldn't we maintain complete control of the facilities and of the grain?

Our agricultural exports have been shifted from what were usually considered "giveaway" programs to commercial transactions. Look at these figures from the U.S. Department of Agriculture, for example:

AGRICULTURAL EXPORTS

YEAR	COMMERCIAL	GOVERNMENT PROGRAMS
1960	$ 3,236,000,000	$1,283,000,000
1976	21,100,000,000	1,047,000,000

We're getting back a lot more hard cash. Foreign countries are forced into paying out real money, and a lot of it, to keep alive.

NORTH OF JOHNSTOWN, COLORADO

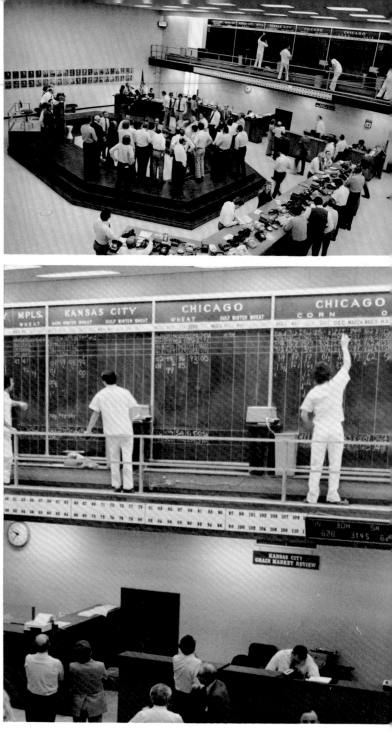

Board of Trade, Kansas City, Missouri.

One result of this is an abrupt shift in our balance of payments. Agricultural exports in 1960 were a net deficit against agricultural imports in the balance of payments; in 1976 they topped $14 billion.

In our not unusual fashion, the United States has avoided making a basic decision, at least consciously. The question is: should the sale of our farm products abroad be left to the laws of supply and demand, or should these sales be used as a political tool?

The answer is, to me, quite clear, though Washington will hem and haw when asked. For many years we gave away, particularly under Public Law 480, food to hungry nations. Washington decided which countries qualified. Today, when cash deals are more the mode, Washington is again calling the tune, though more hesitantly. I think we should recognize, very reluctantly, the necessity for the use of food as a political bargaining tool. I'm not happy to do so; I just feel it's a necessity.

We export a higher percentage of our wheat than of any other major crop we raise. Close to 70 percent of our production is now going abroad. We've helped get the rest of the world hooked on wheat, and that's fortunate, for wheat's likely to be the crop we can expand most readily when necessary.

There's a serious misconception about where our farm exports go abroad. Most Americans think of us as supporting the USSR with our wheat exports, and blame Russians for soaring grain prices here. In 1975, however, Russia ranked only fourteenth among countries receiving our agricultural exports. By 1976, although Russia had jumped to second place, she imported only slightly more than half as much as Japan, and very slightly more than the Netherlands or West Germany.

If we need to produce an increasing amount of farm goods for export, how do we go about it? Miracles may be available for some of the other parts of the world; if other countries can learn to use them, there are many techniques we use that are applicable elsewhere, though many involve sophistication that may be difficult to attain. Most of us are familiar with the "green revolution" which gave India a boost in grain production. Getting such techniques widely adopted is proving difficult, but it should be possible.

In the United States, though, few miracles appear on the horizon. Most farm economists agree we can gradually increase production through increasing input of energy and fertilizer, better seed, and more know-how. But no quantum jumps seem available.

For many crops in the United States, I feel, we have waiting in the wings a major problem we haven't faced up to: water. The limit to production of crops in many areas of the western United States is the availability of water.

A number of areas are in danger of exhausting their existing supplies. We tend to think of irrigation water as being replenished each year by mountain snowfall, and in some sections of the country this is true. In others, we need to think of farming as being possible because the fields are

WINDSOR, COLORADO

108

ABBYVILLE, KANSAS

sitting on top of a giant reservoir that has accumulated over hundreds of thousands of years. We're pulling this longtime accumulation out of the ground in a few years. We will run out of water at some future time in these areas. My own belief is that within ten years this problem will be reshaping farming in some parts of the country.

One proposed solution to starvation is to shift our own food consumption, and that of other "high living" countries, from meat to grain. Currently, if you think about it, much of our farm acreage goes to feed animals, which we then eat. If we short-circuited this, and simply ate the grain (the argument goes) we would have much more food available. The usual figure given is that it takes something between four and ten times as much acreage to get our food by eating animals as it does if we consume the grain directly.

There's clearly some validity to this argument, though maybe not so much as its proponents would like to have us believe. Much of the feed for beef cattle comes from grazing, or from cutting hay, and much of the grazing and hay land is either too dry for crops, or too steep to be cropped. This is, however, a "watering down" of the argument, not a denial.

But it may be difficult to convince the American public that they should alter their diet to support the lives of some unknown in some far off country. A harsh judgment but, I suspect, a valid one.

If this dietary shift can take place through the pricing system—if American meat prices go up as foreign buyers of grain compete with American beef consumers -then laws of supply and demand might eventually force Americans to depend more heavily on protein from grain rather than from animals. But, even if they are starving, can underdeveloped nations afford to price us out of the grain market? I doubt it.

So we may end up enjoying steak while someone on the other side of the globe starves for lack of the grain that went into the steer that provided our steak. In the abstract it's a horrible thought. In practice I think it's likely to happen.

There may be a couple of steps in between. First, if we raise beef without finishing it off with a high quality grain diet, we can radically reduce the number of crop acres involved in each pound of beef, and particularly we can decrease the quality of the acreage used—more dry pastureland, less good cropland.

And second, we have already learned to pad out our meat supplies with substitute protein, usually called TVP, textured vegetable protein. It's already available in most supermarkets as hamburger stretched with soybean protein.

Still, I think we may be munching our hamburgers while we watch the boob tube as the cameras pan across the starving of Africa or Asia. It's not a comforting thought.

Technical Notes

All but two of the pictures in this book were taken either on 4 x 5 sheet film, with a Linhof Technika camera, or on 2¼ x 2¾ format roll film, with a single lens reflex RB 67 camera. The two 35mm. negatives were of the granary weevil insects. Obviously, I use 35 mm. when necessary, but prefer larger film sizes.

This is simply a personal preference. Most photographers working today prefer the 35mm. camera as their standard tool. I don't happen to, and I was born with a husky frame which manages bigger cameras without a hassle.

Our sheet film is tray processed, with inspection as the processing continues. I use a modified version of Ansel Adams' zone system for exposure and processing, a system taught me by John Doscher, at Vermont's Country School of Photography. This system gives negatives with excellent shadow detail, and without blocked-up highlights.

Roll film is unfortunately not adaptable to tray processing or inspection. We use a deep tank and nitrogen burst agitation, a gadget we invented out of frustration with the unevenness of the standard reel processing. Sheet film, unfortunately, still gives us better negative quality than roll film.

Grant Heilman

I say "we" because most of my darkrooming is done by my associates, Barry Runk and Jeanne Chappell. We've worked together a long time and we all recognize that no photograph is better than the negative, and the print that's made from it.

As you have seen in the book, I'm a relatively conservative photographer. I regularly experiment with all the fads that come along, but usually revert to straightforward pictorial quality. I also feel that talking about photography is not so good as looking at it!